# A Story Book of Jesus

*Enid Blyton*

It's wonderful to see that Enid Blyton's inspirational writing is being made available to today's young readers.

Her writing style has the same richness of language that can be found in the King James version of the Bible, so new readers will be treated to not only good stories but her "poetry in voice" as well.

*Tomie dePaola*

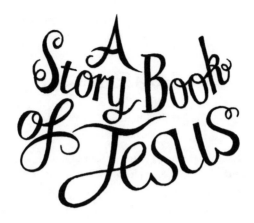

# A Story Book of Jesus

## Enid Blyton

### Illustrated by Norman Young

# ELEMENT
#### CHILDREN'S BOOKS

**SHAFTESBURY, DORSET · BOSTON, MASSACHUSETTS · MELBOURNE, VICTORIA**

*Enid Blyton*™

Text © Enid Blyton Limited 1956
All Rights Reserved

Enid Blyton's signature is a trademark of Enid Blyton Limited
For further information please contact www.blyton.com

First published in Great Britain by Macmillan in 1956
First published by Element Children's Books in 1998,
Shaftesbury, Dorset SP7 8BP
Published in the USA in 1998 by Element Books Inc.
160 North Washington Street, Boston MA 02114

Published in Australia in 1998 by Element Books Limited
and distributed by Penguin Books Australia Ltd,
487 Maroondah Highway, Ringwood, Victoria 3134

British Library Cataloguing in Publication data available.

Library of Congress Cataloging in Publication data available.

ISBN 1 901881 52 0

Cover design by Gabrielle Morton

Cover and endpapers illustrations © Mary Kuper 1998

Inside illustrations © Norman Young 1998

Typeset by Dorchester Typesetting Group Ltd
Printed and bound in Great Britain by Creative Print and Design

# Contents

# *Foreword*

This is a book for mothers and young children; for mothers who want to introduce the story of Jesus in the simplest way to the youngest child; and for young children who are able to read and will enjoy for themselves the wonderful stories of Jesus, the greatest figure the world has even seen.

I have written the stories in simple, straightforward language so that the mother will not continually have to stop to explain the meaning of words or sentences, and so that the child, however young, may listen with understanding and enjoyment. I have used the words of the original text where it is possible, and have kept closely to the Gospel stories, so that when children eventually read them for themselves in the New Testament, they will recognize them with delight as those they have heard almost from their early infancy.

As soon as a child can listen quietly to a tale, he or she should be told the story of Jesus. It is an ideal story for young, developing minds – a tale of great interest and beauty, and with enough of drama to hold the child enthralled from beginning to end. It is also one of the finest ways of instilling in children such precepts as "Love one another," and of teaching them that goodness, kindness, unselfishness, and justice are among the greatest things in the world. Example is one of the soundest ways of teaching these virtues – and in Jesus the child has a perfect hero to follow: a man of complete integrity; of boundless kindness; just, fearless, and merciful; the son of God, able to heal bodies as well as souls, bringing a message of love that has sounded down the centuries. He is also the friend of every child, and a storyteller that the children of his day must have been enthralled to hear. To our own young children he can seem very near, very loving, and very lovable.

I like to think of the thousands of children who will sit close to their mothers, hearing them read the wonderful old stories, at the same time gazing with delight on the lovely pictures that bring the tales to life. I hope that those same children will remember for years the simple stories and the delightful illustrations that accompany them.

*Enid Blyton*

# Chapter 1

*The First Christmas*

Nearly two thousand years ago there lived in the town of Nazareth in Palestine a girl called Mary. One day an angel came to her with great news.

"Hail, Mary!" said the angel. "I bring you great tidings. You will have a little baby boy, and you must call him Jesus. He shall be great, and shall be called the Son of the Highest. He will be the Son of God, and of his kingdom there shall be no end."

Now Mary was only a village girl, and she could hardly believe this news, but as she gazed up at the angel, she knew it was true. She was full of joy and wonder. She was to have a baby boy of her own, and he was to be the little Son of God.

Mary married a carpenter called Joseph, and together they lived in a little house on the hillside. Her heart sang as she thought of the tiny baby who was to come to her that winter.

The summer went by, and it was fall. Then the winter came – and with it arrived men who put up a big notice in the town. Mary went to read it.

It was a notice saying that all people must go to their own home-town and pay taxes. This meant that Mary and Joseph must leave Nazareth, and go to Bethlehem, for that was where their families had once lived.

"You shall ride on the donkey," said Joseph. "I will walk beside you. We shall be three or four days on the way, but the little donkey will take you easily."

So Mary and Joseph set off to go to Bethlehem. Mary rode on the little donkey, and Joseph walked beside her, leading it. Many other people were on the roads too, for all had to go to pay their taxes. Mary and Joseph traveled for some days, and one night Mary felt very tired.

"When shall we be there?" said Mary. "I feel tired. I want to lie down and rest."

"There are the lights of Bethlehem," said Joseph, pointing through the darkness to where some lights twinkled on a hilltop. "We shall soon be there."

"Shall we find room at Bethlehem?" said Mary. "There are so many people going there."

"We will go to an inn," said Joseph. "There you will find warmth and food, comfort and rest."

When they climbed up the hill to the town of Bethlehem, Mary felt so tired that she longed to go to the inn at once.

"Here it is," said Joseph, and he stopped the little donkey before a building that was well-lit. Joseph called for the innkeeper, and a man came to the door, holding up a lantern so that he might see the travelers.

"Can you give us a room quickly?" said Joseph. "My wife is very tired, and needs to rest at once."

"My inn is full, and there is not a bed to be had in the whole town," said the innkeeper. "You will find nowhere to sleep. There is no room at the inn."

"Can't you find us a resting-place somewhere?" said Joseph, anxiously. "My wife has come far and is so tired."

The man swung his lantern up to look at Mary, who sat patiently on the donkey, waiting. He saw how tired she was, how white her face looked, and how patiently she sat there. He was filled with pity, and he wondered what he could do.

"I have a cave at the back of my inn, where my oxen sleep," he said. "Your wife could lie there. I will have it swept for you and new straw put down. But that is the best I can offer you."

So Joseph said they would sleep in the cave that night, and he helped Mary off the donkey. She walked wearily round to the cave in the hillside, and saw the servant putting down piles of clean straw for her.

Mary lay down in the straw. Joseph looked after her tenderly. He brought her milk to drink, he made her a pillow of a rug, and he hung his cloak over the doorway so that the wind could be kept away.

Their little donkey was with them in the stable too. He ate his supper hungrily, looking round at Mary and Joseph as he munched the hay. Mary smelt the nearby oxen, and felt the warmth their bodies made.

And that night Jesus was born to Mary, in the little stable at Bethlehem. Mary held him closely in her arms, looking at him with joy and love. The oxen looked around too, and the little donkey stared with large eyes. The doves watched and cooed softly. The little son of God was there!

"Joseph, bring me the clothes I had with me," said Mary. "I thought perhaps the baby would be born while we traveled and I brought his swaddling-clothes with me."

In those far-off days the first clothes a baby wore were called swaddling-clothes. He was wrapped around and around in a long piece of linen cloth. Mary took the linen from Joseph, and wrapped the baby in his swaddling-clothes. Then she wondered where to put him, for she wanted to sleep.

"He cannot lie on this straw," said Mary, anxiously. "Oh, Joseph, we have no cradle for our little baby."

"See," said Joseph, "there is a manger here full of soft hay. It will be a cradle for him."

Joseph put the tiny child into the manger, laying him down carefully in the soft hay. How small he was! How downy his hair was, and how tiny his fingers were with their pink nails!

Then Mary, tired out, fell asleep on the straw, while Joseph kept watch beside her, and  the baby slept peacefully in the manger nearby. The lantern light flickered when the wind stole in, and sometimes the oxen stamped on the floor.

That was the first Christmas, the birthday of the little Christ-child. The little son of God was born, the great teacher of the world – but only Joseph and Mary knew that at last he had come.

No bells rang out at his birth. The people in the inn slept soundly, not guessing that the son of God was in a nearby stable.

But the angels in heaven knew the great happening. They must spread the news. They must come to our world and tell someone. They had kept watch over the city of Bethlehem that night, and they were filled with joy to know that the little son of God was born.

# Chapter 2

*The Shepherds in the Night*

Who was awake to hear the angels' news? There was no one in the town awake that night, but on the hillside outside Bethlehem there were some shepherds, watching their sheep.

They spoke quietly together. They had much to talk about that night, for they had watched hundreds of people walking and riding by their quiet fields, on the way to pay their taxes at Bethlehem. It was seldom that the shepherds saw so many people.

As the shepherds talked, looking around at their quiet sheep, a very strange thing happened. The sky became bright, and a great light appeared in it, and shone all around them. The shepherds were surprised and frightened. What was this brilliant light that shone in the darkness of the night?

They looked up fearfully. Then in the middle of the dazzling light they saw a beautiful angel. He shone too, and he spoke to them in a voice that sounded like mighty music.

"See," said one shepherd to another in wonder. "An angel!"

They all fell upon their knees, and some covered their faces with their cloaks, afraid of the dazzling light. They were trembling.

Then the voice of the angel came upon the hillside, full of joy and happiness.

"Fear not; for behold I bring you good tidings of great joy, which shall be to all people. For unto you is born this day in the city of David a savior, which is Christ the Lord. And this shall be a sign unto you – you shall find the babe wrapped in swaddling-clothes and lying in a manger."

The shepherds listened in the greatest wonder. They gazed at the angel in awe, and listened to this wonderful being with his great overshadowing wings. As they looked, another strange thing happened, which made the shepherds tremble even more.

The dark sky disappeared, and in its place came a crowd of shining beings, bright as the sun, filling the whole sky. Everywhere the shepherds looked there were angels, singing joyfully.

"Glory to God in the highest," sang the host of angels, "and on earth peace, goodwill towards men."

Over and over again the angels sang these words, and the shepherds, amazed, afraid, and wondering, listened and marveled. Surely all the angels in heaven were over Bethlehem that night.

Then, as the shepherds watched, the dazzling light slowly faded away, and the darkness of the night came back. The angels vanished with the light, and then the sky was quite dark again, set with twinkling stars that had been outshone by the glory of the angels. A sheep bleated and a dog barked. There was nothing to show that heaven had opened to the shepherds that night.

The frightened men were silent for a time, and then they began to talk in low voices that gradually became louder.

"They were angels. How dazzling they were! We saw angels. They came to us, the shepherds on the hillside."

"It couldn't have been a dream. Nobody could dream like that."

"I was frightened. I hardly dared to look at the angels at first."

"Why did they come to us? Why should they choose men like us to sing to?"

"You heard what the first angel said – he said a savior had been born to us, Christ the Lord. He said that he was born in the city of David tonight – that means in Bethlehem, for Bethlehem is the city of David!"

"Can it be true?"

"We will go and find the little king. I want to see him."

"We cannot go at midnight. And how do we know where he is?"

"Why should the holy child be put in a manger? Surely he should have a cradle!"

"He must have been born to one of the late travelers, who could find no room at the inn. They must have had to put him in a manger. I am going to see."

The shepherds, excited and full of great wonder, went up the hillside to Bethlehem. They left their dogs to guard the sheep, all but one who went with them.

Soon they came to the inn, and, at the back, where the stable was built into the hillside cave, they saw a light. "Let us go to the stable and see if the son of God is there," whispered one shepherd. So, treading softly, they went round to the back of the inn, and came to the entrance of the stable. Across it was stretched Joseph's rough cloak to keep out the wind. The shepherds peered over it into the stable.

They saw what the angel had told them – a babe wrapped in swaddling-clothes, lying in a manger!

On the straw, asleep, was Mary. Nearby was Joseph, keeping watch over her and the child.

"There's the baby," whispered the shepherds, in excitement. "In the manger, wrapped in swaddling-clothes. There is the savior, the little son of God."

Mary heard what they said. She lifted the child from the manger and took him on her knee. The shepherds knelt down before him and worshiped him. Again and again they told the wondering Mary all that had happened.

The oxen stared, and the dog pressed close to his master, wondering at the strange happenings of the night. Then, seeing that Mary was tired, the shepherds went at last, walking softly in the darkness.

"We will tell everyone the news tomorrow!" said the shepherds. "Everyone. What will they say when they know that while they slept we have seen angels?"

Down the hill they went, back to their sheep, sometimes looking up into the sky to see if an angel might once again appear. All through that night they talked eagerly of the angels, the holy child in the stable, and of Mary, his gentle mother.

The next day they told everyone of what had happened to them in the night, and many people went to peep in at the stable, to see the little child.

Mary held him close to her, and thought often of the angel she herself had seen nine months before. She thought of the excited shepherds, and the host of shining angels they too had seen and heard. Her baby was the little son of God. Mary could hardly believe such a thing was true.

# Chapter 3

## *The Three Wise Men*

And by the light of that same star
Three wise men came from country far.
To seek for a king was their intent,
And to follow the star wherever it went.

Far far away from Bethlehem, in a land that lay to the east, there lived some wise and learnèd men. At night these men studied the stars in the heavens. They said that the stars showed them the great thoughts of God. They said that when a new star appeared, it was God's way of telling men that some great thing was happening in the world.

Then, one night, when the wise men were watching, a new star appeared in the sky. The second night the star was brighter still. The third night it was so dazzling that its light seemed to put out the twinkling of the other stars.

"God has sent this star to say that something wonderful is happening," said the wise men. "We will look in our old, old books, where wisdom is kept, and we will find out what this star means."

So they studied their old wise books, and they found in them a tale of a great king who was to be born into the world to rule over it. He was to be King of the Jews, and ruler of the world.

"The star seems to stand over Israel, the kingdom of the Jews," said one wise man. "This star must mean that the great king is born at last. We will go to worship him, for our books say he will be the greatest king in the world."

"We will take him presents of gold and frankincense and myrrh," said another. "We will tell our servants to make ready to go with us."

So, a little while later, when the star was still brilliant every night in the sky, the three wise men set off on their camels. They were like kings in their own country, and a long train of servants followed behind on swift-footed camels. They traveled for many days and nights, and always at night the great star shone before them to guide them on their way.

They came at last to the land of Israel, where the little Jesus had been born. They went, of course, to the city where the Jewish king lived, thinking that surely the new little king would be there, in the palace of Jerusalem.

Herod was the king there, and he was a wicked man. When his servants came running to tell him that three rich men, seated on magnificent camels, with a train of servants behind them, were at the gates of the palace, Herod bade his servants bring them before him.

The wise men went to see Herod. They looked strange and most kingly in their turbans and flowing robes. They asked Herod a question that amazed and angered him.

"Where is the child who is born King of the Jews?" they asked. "His star has gone before us in the east, and we have brought presents for him, and we wish to worship him. Where is he?"

"I am the king," said Herod, full of anger. "What is this child you talk of? And what is this star?"

The wise men told him all they knew. "We are certain that a great king has been born," they said, "and we must find him. Can you not tell us where he is?"

Herod sat silent for a moment. Who was this new-born king of whom these rich strangers spoke? Herod was quite certain they were speaking the truth. He could see that these men were learnèd, and knew far more than he did.

"I will find out where this new-born king is, and kill him," thought Herod to himself. "But this I will not tell these men. They shall go to find the child for me, and tell me where he is – then I will send my soldiers to kill him."

So Herod spoke craftily to the wise men. "I will find out what you want to know. I have wise men in my court who know the sayings of long-ago Jews, who said that in due time a great king would be born. Perhaps this is the child you mean."

Then Herod sent for his own wise men and bade them look in the books they had, to see what was said of a great king to be born to the Jews. The learnèd men looked and they found what they wanted to know.

"The king will be born in the city of Bethlehem," they said.

"Where is that?" asked the wise men.

"Not far away," said Herod. "It will not take you long to get there."

"We will go now," said the three wise men, and they turned to go. But Herod stopped them.

"Wait," he said. "When you find this new-born king, come back here to tell me where he is, for I too want to worship him."

The wise men did not know that Herod meant to kill the little king, not worship him. "You shall be told where he is," they said. "We will return here and tell you."

Then they mounted their camels and went to find the city of Bethlehem, which, as Herod had said, was not far away.

The sun set, and once again the brilliant star flashed into the sky. It seemed to stand exactly over the town of Bethlehem. The strangers, with their train of servants, went up the hill to the town, their harnesses jingling and their jeweled turbans and cloaks flashing in the brilliant light of the great star.

They passed the wondering shepherds, and went into

the little city. They stopped to ask a woman to guide them. "Can you tell us where to find a new-born child?" they said.

The woman stared at these rich strangers in surprise. She felt sure they must want to know where Jesus was, for everyone knew how angels had come to proclaim his birth.

"Yes," she said, "you will find the baby in the house yonder. He was born in the stable, because there was no room for him in the inn – but now that the travelers have left the city, room was found for his parents at that

house. You will find him there with his mother."

The star seemed to stand right over the house to which the woman pointed. The wise men felt sure it was the right one. They made their way to it, riding on their magnificent camels.

# Chapter 4

*The Warning of the Angel*

When Mary saw these three grandly dressed men kneeling before her tiny baby, she was amazed. Angels had come to proclaim his birth, shepherds had worshiped him – and now here were three great men kneeling before him.

"We have found the little king," said one wise man. "We have brought him kingly presents. Here is gold for him, a gift for a king."

"And here is sweet-smelling frankincense," said another.

"And I bring him myrrh, rare and precious," said the third.

These were indeed kingly gifts, and Mary looked at them in wonder, holding the baby closely against her. He was her own child, but he seemed to belong to many others too – to the angels in heaven, to the simple shepherds in the fields, to wise and rich men of far countries. He had been born for the whole world, not only for her.

The wise men left and went to stay for the night at the inn. There was room for them, because the many

travelers who had come to the little city had left some time before.

"Tomorrow we will go back to Herod and tell him where the new-born king is, so that he may come and worship him," said the wise men. But in the night God sent dreams to them, to warn them not to return to Herod, but to go back to their country another way.

So they mounted their camels, and returned to their country without going near Jerusalem, where Herod lived.

In vain Herod waited for the three wise men to return. His servants soon found out that they had been to Bethlehem but had returned home another way. This made Herod so angry that he hardly knew what he was doing.

First he sent his soldiers after the wise men to stop

them, but they were too far away. Then he made up his
mind to find the new-born baby and kill him.

But no one knew where the child was, nor did anyone
even know how old he might be. The wise men themselves had not known how old the baby was. Herod sat
on his throne, his heart black and angry.

"Call my soldiers to me," he said at last.

They came before him, and Herod gave them a cruel
and terrible command.

"Go to the town of Bethlehem and kill every boychild
there who is under two years old," he said. "Go to the
villages round about and kill the young baby boys there
too. Let no one escape."

The soldiers rode off, their harnesses jingling loudly.
They rode up the hill to Bethlehem, and once again the
quiet shepherds stared in wonder at strange visitors. But
soon, alas, they heard the screams and cries of the
mothers whose little sons had been killed, and they knew
that something dreadful was happening.

Every boy-child was killed by the cruel soldiers, and
when their terrible work was done, they rode down the
hills again, past the watching shepherds, to tell Herod
that his commands had been obeyed.

"There is no boy-child under two years old left in
Bethlehem or the villages nearby," said the captain of the
soldiers, and Herod was well pleased.

"The new-born king is dead," he thought. "I have been

clever. I have killed the baby who might one day have been greater than I am."

But Jesus was not killed. He was safe. On the night that the wise men had left Mary, the little family had gone to bed, and were asleep. But, as Joseph slept, an angel came to him in his dreams, and spoke to him.

"Arise," said the shining angel. "Take the young child and his mother, and flee into Egypt, and stay there until I tell you to return; for Herod will seek the young child to destroy him."

Joseph awoke at once. He sat up. The angel was gone, but the words he had said still sounded in Joseph's ears. Joseph knew that there was danger near, and he awoke Mary.

"We must make ready and go," he said, and he told her what the angel had said. Then Mary knew they must leave, and she went to put her few things into a bundle, and to lift up the baby Jesus. Joseph went to get the little donkey, and soon, in the silence of the night, the four of them fled away secretly.

They went as quickly as they could, longing to pass over into the land of Egypt, which did not belong to Herod. He would have no power over them there.

So, when Herod's soldiers came a little later to the city of Bethlehem, Jesus was not there. He was safe in Egypt, where Herod could not reach him.

And there, until it was safe for him to return to his

own country, the little new-born king lived and grew strong and kind and loving. No one knew he was a king. His father was a carpenter, and his friends were the boys of the villages around.

But his mother knew. Often she remembered the tale of the shepherds who had seen the angels in the sky, and she remembered too the three wise men who had come to kneel before her baby. She still had the wonderful presents they had given to her for him. He would one day be the greatest king in the world.

But it was not by power or riches or might that the baby in the stable grew to be the greatest man the world has ever seen. It was by something greater than all these – by *love* alone.

That is the story of the first Christmas, which we remember to this day, and which we keep with joy and delight.

# Chapter 5

## *The Little Boy Jesus*

Mary and Joseph did not go back to their own country until an angel had told them it was safe to do so.

"Arise," said the angel, "and take the young child and his mother, and go back to your own land; for they are dead who wanted to kill your child."

So Mary and Joseph packed all their things, saddled their little donkey, and set off back to their own land.

"We will go to the town of Nazareth," said Joseph. "Our friends are there. We shall be happy in that place."

And so one day the little company arrived at Nazareth, set high up on the green hillside.

"Now we are home again," said Mary, gladly, "See how the little white houses shine in the sun. We will have one of those to live in, Joseph, and our little Jesus shall grow up here in the sunshine, and learn to help you in your shop."

So Jesus was brought up in one of the little white houses on the hillside. It was made of sun-dried bricks, and he helped Joseph to whitewash it each year, so that it shone clean and white.

In this little house Joseph set up his carpenter's shop.
Mary and Jesus liked to hear all the hammering and
sawing that went on. Jesus often went into the shop and
watched his father. He sometimes lifted a heavy hammer,
and played with the big and little nails.

"One day I will help you," he told Joseph. "I shall be a
carpenter too."

Jesus did all the things that the other children of
Nazareth did. He went to fetch water from the well for
his mother in the old stone pitcher. Even today the
people of Nazareth see the same old well, where once,
years ago, a bright-eyed boy called Jesus came to fetch
water and to talk to the other children there.

Jesus wandered over the hillside too, and picked

flowers for his mother. The hillside was covered with
them in spring and summer. Jesus talked with the shepherds, and heard their tales. He played with the lambs,
listened to the birds singing, and watched the sower
sowing his seed in the fields.

His mother told him many stories. You know them
too. She told him how God made the world. He heard
about the Garden of Eden and how Adam and Eve were
sent away from it. He liked hearing about Noah and his
ark, and he loved the rainbow when he saw it in the sky,
and remembered how God had set it there as a promise
never to flood the world again.

He knew the stories of the giant Samson, of David
and Goliath, and Daniel in the lions' den. Mary taught
him to obey God's commands, and to pray to him each
day. Jesus listened eagerly, and learned everything his
mother could tell him.

When he was old enough he, like you, went to school.
He had to learn his lessons – and he had to learn something else too. He had to learn the law of God, and this
was very difficult.

The law of God had been written down by Jewish
teachers, and they had filled books full of tiny laws as
well as big ones. The tiny laws told people exactly how
they should wash a plate, and arrange their clothes, and
things like that. When Jesus saw that the people sometimes thought more of doing these small things correctly

than they did of such big things as being kind and generous to one another, he was puzzled.

"Surely it is better to be like old Sarah, who lives down the hill and is always kind to everyone in trouble, though she forgets the little commands – than it is to be like James, who never forgets the little things, but is unjust and unkind all the time," thought Jesus.

He was only a boy then, but he thought things out for himself. He prayed to God to show him what was really right and good.

"One day I shall know these things," he said to himself. "I shall know enough to tell others what I think. I shall be able to teach them and help them. That is the thing I want to do most of all."

# Chapter 6

*Twelve Years Old*

Once each year the Jewish people kept a great feast or holiday. They liked to go to Jerusalem, where their beautiful Temple was built. Joseph and Mary loved to go too.

"What do you do there when you go?" asked Jesus.

"There are meetings and services," said Mary. "And we meet many people there, and see old friends. It is an exciting and happy time. When you are twelve we will take you with us, Jesus."

So, when he was twelve years old, his mother kept her promise. "You can come with us," she said. "You are a big boy now – you have learned the law of God, and it is time that you went to the Temple with us and became one of the members of the Church. You must promise to keep the law, you know."

It was very exciting to think of such a long journey. Jesus had heard so much of Jerusalem and the Temple. Now he was really going to see it.

"I shall walk down strange roads, I shall see hundreds of people. At night we shall camp out by the wayside, and see the stars shining above us," he thought. "And perhaps I shall be able to talk to learnèd and wise men in the Temple and ask them some of the things I want so much to know."

The great day came. Joseph and Mary were ready to go. Joseph had finished all the work he had to do and Mary had tidied up the house. Everything was ready. Joseph shut the door of the little house, and smiled to see Jesus' excited face.

Other children were going too. They ran to join Jesus. They all liked this wise, kindly boy and the things he said and did.

"Walk with us!" they cried. "We're going down the hill and across the plain – and then we cross the River Jordan. Come along!"

It was a lovely journey over the hills and plains to Jerusalem. Jesus felt the spring sun warm on his shoulders, he heard the birds singing, and saw the thousands of pretty flowers under his feet.

There was plenty to see on the way. Each day was exciting – and the nights were even more exciting, for then camp fires were made, meals were cooked, and old songs and hymns were sung by the hundreds of people in the little camps.

Jesus liked to watch all the lights from the camp fires. He liked to lie on his back and look up at the brilliant stars. He liked to hear the singing.

Then at last they came to Jerusalem, and went to the

Holy Temple. Jesus stood and looked at the beautiful building.

"That is the house of God, my heavenly father," he thought. "He dwells there. I am going to his house."

Jesus was taken into the Temple. God seemed very near to him there. He was taken before the wise men of the Temple, and they made him a member of the Church – a Disciple of the Law, as they called it.

"Now you must count yourself grown-up," said the wise men. "You must keep all the laws of the Church."

And then the great feast was over. The holiday was ended. It was time to go home.

"Here are our things for you to carry, Joseph," said Mary. "How lovely it has been to meet all our old friends again! How good to know that Jesus belongs to our Church! And how nice it will be to be back home again in our own little house!"

Mary did not see Jesus all that day. She wondered where he was. Perhaps he was with the other boys. She must think of him as grown-up now, and let him go away on his own. But where could he be?

"He is sure to come and look for us when we camp tonight," she thought. But the night came, and there was no Jesus.

"We must look for him, Joseph," said Mary, anxiously. "Go and ask the other boys if they know where he is."

"No," said the boys. "We haven't seen him at all. He didn't walk with us."

Nobody knew where Jesus was. Not one person had seen him since they had left Jerusalem. Mary and Joseph were very worried.

"We will go back to Jerusalem," said Joseph. So back they went. But still they could not find Jesus. He was not at the house where they had stayed. Nobody could tell them anything about him.

Jerusalem was a big city. Mary and Joseph hardly knew where to look. For three days they went up and down the streets, asking everyone they met the same question. "Have you seen our boy Jesus?"

"There is only one place left to look," said Mary, at last. "And that is the Temple itself. Jesus loved the Temple, Joseph. He wanted to ask the wise men so many questions, and there was no time. Perhaps he has gone back to the Temple."

They went to see – and there in the Temple they found Jesus. He had not been wandering about the great city, playing, or looking at the strange sights. He had been in the Temple all the time, an earnest, urgent little boy, anxious to find out all he could about God and his commands.

He had found the wise men, the ones who knew more about the Jewish law than anyone in the land. He had asked them questions – questions they did not know

how to answer! They were amazed at this young boy who knew so much about the law of God – it seemed that he knew more than they did!

They kept him there hour after hour, asking him questions too. Jesus forgot everything except that now at last he was finding out things he needed to know. He felt close to God in the Temple, he felt that his heavenly father had welcomed him, that he was really and truly his son.

Perhaps in those three strange days, when he was talking so earnestly with the wise and learnèd men, Jesus felt for the first time his great power for doing good. He listened to all the wise men said, turning their long words into simple ones in his mind, seeing how easy it would be to tell the common people these things in simple language and stories.

Here, in the Temple, he belonged to God, more than he belonged to Joseph and Mary. He stood there in the midst of all the wise men, and they marveled at his knowledge and wisdom.

And then he suddenly saw his parents nearby, looking at him with anxious, troubled eyes! Mary went to him, weeping with joy.

"Son!" she said. "Why have you behaved like this? Your father and I have been looking for you everywhere. We have been so worried."

Jesus was surprised. "But did you not guess where I would be?" he said. "I had to come to my father's house, and learn the things I should know."

He went home with Mary and Joseph. He became their young boy again, and obeyed them in all things. He was wise and he was wonderful, but the time had not yet come when he could do exactly as he wanted to.

So he settled down again in Nazareth, and pondered over all the things he had learned in the Temple. He knew that wisdom and understanding could only grow slowly, and he was content to live with his family, helping his father and mother, until the right time came.

# Chapter 7

## *Jesus Grows Up*

When he was twelve years old, Jesus began to help Joseph, his father, in the shop. He had always liked to play with hammer and nails, but now he had to learn how to be a real carpenter.

"You can try to mend this," Joseph would say to him, when someone brought a broken bench.

"See – this leg is no good. Make a new one and fit it in properly, as you have so often seen me do."

Jesus liked working with his hands. He could think as he worked, and it was pleasant up in the little white house on the hills, with the door wide open to the sun, and the birds singing outside.

Jesus sawed and hammered, and thought long thoughts as he worked. He remembered all he had learned from his teachers. He remembered what the priests at the Temple had told him. He thought about God the Father, and how great and good he was. Then he thought sadly how unkind and unjust and cruel so many people were.

"There is Simon – he speaks so roughly to his old mother. And Martha, who hits her little brother, and Thomas, who never tells the truth. Why do they do these things? How sad the great father God must be to see his children on earth being cruel and unkind!"

As he worked with his tools, Jesus began to wish that he could go out into the world and tell the people all the things he thought about. If only they were told, perhaps they would believe, and be good and kind!

"It is goodness and kindness and justice that matter so much," thought the growing Jesus. "If we all loved one another and were good to one another, there would be no more wars, no more unhappiness, no more cruelty. One day I must tell everyone these things. That is really my work, the work I must do."

But for a long time Jesus stayed at home and did not go out into the world to preach and teach, as he so much wanted to do. He knew that until he could feel only goodness in his own heart, and could be sure that not one bad thing was in him, he was not ready to teach others. He must work, and think, and pray, and he must grow wiser and wiser until the right time came.

"The son of Joseph the carpenter will grow into a good man," said the people of Nazareth to one another.

"We love him," said the children.

"He does good work," said the men. "He never shirks his job. We may be sure that whatever we ask him to make or to mend, he will do well and honestly. He is a fine workman."

"He is a good son," thought his mother, Mary, gazing at him as she so often did, and marveling at the goodness in his face, and the wise things he said. She remembered the angels who sang at his birth. What would he grow into, this wise, thoughtful son of hers?

Through those long years of boyhood, when Jesus was slowly growing into a man, he taught himself all the things he wanted to teach other people.

"If I teach good things I must be good myself," he thought. "God, my heavenly father, will help me. I will pray to him often, and he will give me the wisdom and goodness and power that I shall need when I go out into the world."

So Jesus grew from boyhood into manhood, and now was a man, a carpenter like his father. Everyone trusted him and liked him. Joseph was proud of this son of his, so fair and just and wise.

Surely the time was coming near when Jesus might leave his work with hammer and saw, and go out into the world and preach?

No. It was not yet time. Joseph died, and Mary turned to Jesus in her sorrow. Jesus could not leave her then. He must comfort her, work for her and be with her.

He was thirty years old when the time came for him to leave Nazareth and go out to teach people all the things he knew. He was a man, wise and full of a great heavenly power, a power that would help him to do miracles and wonders.

"I am going out into the world to found a kingdom of love," he told his wondering mother. "I must save the world from sin and shame and cruelty. I must give it love and goodness instead."

And so Jesus left the little white house on the hills of Nazareth, and went out into the world – the son of God come down to the earth, ready to preach the goodness of his heavenly father, and to do at last the work that he had dreamed of for so many, many years.

# Chapter 8

*Jesus Meets his Cousin John*

Jesus had a cousin called John. He was older than Jesus, but he too had thought long thoughts, he too wanted to be good and to tell others they must leave their bad ways and be good.

John was a strange fellow, fierce and fearless and honest, dressed in a rough coat of camel's hair, tied round with a leather belt. He walked about the countryside, preaching and talking to everyone who would listen.

The children followed him about. They thought he must be a wild man. "What do you eat?" asked one boy, timidly. "You have no home and no money. Do you starve?"

"I eat the honey that the wild bees make," said John. "And when those great insects the locusts fly down, I eat those too."

When people came to John and told him that they had listened to his words, and wanted to do good, he told them that they must show everyone that they had promised this.

"Come with me to the River Jordan," said John. "Let me take you right into the water, so that its waves may

wash over you. Let everyone come and see you in the
river, and hear me say that just as the water washes
away dirt and makes you clean, so will you yourself
wash away the bad things in your heart, and make it
clean and ready for good things to come there instead."

Then all the people who wanted to make their hearts
clean, and to promise to do right, went to the river with
John. He baptized them in the water, and when they
came out they felt that their sins had been washed away,
and that they could begin life again and be good and
kind.

The people called Jesus' cousin John the Baptist,
because he led them to the river and baptized them.

"This John the Baptist is a great man," they said to
one another.

"He is not afraid of anyone," said a woman. "If he sees
someone doing wrong he tells them so. I heard him tell
even the soldiers that they were not to be cruel."

"In our holy book it says that one day the son of God
will come to us," said a man. "Perhaps John is he –
perhaps he is the one we look for?"

"No, I am not," said John. "Wait until the son of God
comes to you and you will see that he is mightier than I
am. I am not fit to do up his shoes!"

And then one day Jesus came to the River Jordan. He
had heard of his great cousin and he had come to talk to
him. John knew him at once. There was such goodness

in Jesus' face that he gazed at him in awe and wonder.

"Behold!" said John. "Behold the Lamb of God!"

"I come to be baptized by you," Jesus said to him.

"You have no sins to be washed away," said John. "You should baptize me, not I you."

But he led Jesus into the water and baptized him as he wished. And then a strange thing happened.

As Jesus came up out of the water the sky opened, and a bright light shone forth. The spirit of God, the heavenly father, flew down in the shape of a dove, and seemed to rest on the glistening wet head of Jesus.

And a voice came down from heaven.

"This is my beloved son, in whom I am well pleased."

# Chapter 9

*Satan, the Prince of Evil*

Jesus heard the voice from heaven. He saw the sky open and the bright light shine. He saw the dove that came down, and knew that it was from God.

He was amazed and awed at what the voice had said: "This is my beloved son."

He knew then that God had chosen him to do his work. He was only a village carpenter, but God thought him worthy to be his own beloved Son.

"I must go into the lonely countryside and think what these things mean," said Jesus to himself. "I know myself what I want to do – and now that God, my heavenly father, has spoken to me, and proclaimed me as his beloved son, I can perhaps do greater things than I thought."

So he went into the countryside, and wandered about, forgetting to eat, lost in thought. He was making his plans. He must go to people everywhere and talk to them in simple words. He would bring peace to the sorrowful. He would try to heal those who were sick. Yes, he might even do that, with God's help!

"I shall fight evil wherever I see it. I shall bring a

kingdom of love into the world," thought Jesus.

But Satan was nearby – Satan, the Prince of Evil, the enemy of all things good and wise. He saw Jesus in the lonely countryside, and looked into his heart. He saw what great goodness and wisdom and power were there, and he was afraid.

"Perhaps I can tempt this man to use his power in the wrong ways," thought Satan. "When people are powerful they become proud and arrogant. Great power makes them so. I will tempt this man to use his power wrongly. He will be able to do miracles of goodness – I will tempt him to do miracles that have no goodness in them!"

So he went and whispered in Jesus' ear.

"You are hungry! You, the son of God, are hungry! Then why do you not turn these stones into bread, and eat?"

But Jesus took no notice. He would never use his power for himself, only for others.

Then Satan put another thought into Jesus' head. It seemed for a moment as if he were standing on the topmost pinnacle of the holy temple at Jerusalem.

"See how easy it would be to show everyone your great powers," whispered Satan. "You want people to know that you are the son of God, don't you? You want people to believe in you? Then throw yourself down from this high pinnacle in front of everyone! God's angels will take care of you, you will not be hurt, and

everyone will marvel, and believe!"

But still Jesus would not listen. So Satan tried once more. He took Jesus to a high mountain, and showed him all the kingdoms and all the greatness of the world lying there before him.

"Do you see all those kingdoms, with their riches and their greatness?" whispered Satan. "They are all yours if you will use your great powers for me and not for God. Follow me as so many others do – I will make you the greatest ruler of the world!"

And then Jesus turned round to Satan and said: "Get you behind me, Satan! I will worship the Lord my God and serve only him!"

Then Satan fled away, defeated. Jesus was glad and his heart was full of joy. He had conquered the Prince of Evil for ever, and was indeed the son of God.

"Now I can do my work," he said. "Now I can use my power for good. The time has come."

And he left the lonely countryside and went out into the world to begin his wonderful work.

# Chapter 10

*Jesus Chooses his Friends*

Now at last the time had come for Jesus to preach to the people, and to help them in all the many ways he could.

But it would be difficult for one man alone to do this. "I must have friends who will help me," thought Jesus. "I must have disciples – men I can teach so that they may themselves go out and teach others. But they must be good men, men I can love and trust."

He went to walk beside the lovely lake of Galilee. Fishermen were at work there, some fishing, some mending nets, and some mending their boats. Jesus watched them, looking closely at each man's face as he passed by.

He saw a boat in which were two brothers, Simon and Andrew. They were good men and good fishermen. Their faces were open and honest. Jesus felt sure he could trust men like these.

He called to them across the shimmering blue water. "Come with me!" he said. "I will make you fishers of men!"

This was a strange thing to say, and Simon and

Andrew did not understand the words at all. Not for some time did they know that Jesus meant them to go out with him and catch men to bring them into his kingdom of love. Now they stood up in their boat and looked at the man who called to them.

There was something in his face that made them go to him. Such goodness shone out of it that they felt they must do what this man said. They rowed to the shore at once and joined Jesus.

There were two other brothers in another boat, mending their nets. Jesus called to them as well. "Come with me!"

The two brothers came eagerly to this man with the beautiful face. Now Jesus had four friends to help him, four good men to do as he said, and to love him and trust him.

He needed twelve, so he chose eight more. But the four he had chosen first always remained the closest to him.

One of them was an eager, lovable man, a man who could be kind and brave and loving – but he could be untrustworthy too, and do things he was ashamed of afterwards. That was Simon – and Jesus knew both the good and the bad in Simon, but he loved him and knew that the good would be more powerful than the bad.

Jesus looked at Simon. "Your name is Simon," he said, "but I shall call your Peter."

"Why is that?" asked Simon, surprised.

"Because the name Peter means a rock," said Jesus. "I have a great kingdom to build, Peter, and it must be built on rock, not sand. You shall be Peter, a rock, and my kingdom will depend a great deal on you."

The twelve disciples followed Jesus everywhere, loving him and worshiping him, a very happy company of men.

# Chapter 11

*Around the Countryside With Jesus*

Jesus began his great and wonderful work. Soon his name was on everyone's lips.

"Have you heard what the man Jesus says? You should go to hear him preach!"

"You can understand every single word he says! He speaks so simply. He tells us that God is our heavenly father who loves us and cares for us. He says we are to trust him and fear nothing."

"We must turn from evil to do good. We must pray and be kind and loving. I have never heard such preaching before."

"The children love him! They follow him everywhere. He tells such wonderful stories, you see, that even the little ones can understand. My little boy is always going to hear him."

"Don't you think his face is goodness itself? Goodness should only be preached by a man like that. The other preachers I have heard never make me want to be good as this man does. It's because he's so good himself."

"Do you know who he is? He's only Jesus, the son of the carpenter at Nazareth! And yet he is greater and better than anyone I have ever known!"

So the people talked of him, loving him, crowding to hear him in the churches when he preached, gathering around him on the hills when he talked to them, bringing their children to him because he loved them and understood them.

And then other things began to be said.

"Listen! Have you heard what Jesus did to old Anna? You know she was so ill? Well, he touched her and made her better! She is walking about again!"

"Have you heard about little John? His foot was always bad, and he couldn't walk on it. His mother took him to Jesus, and he took the boy into his arms and stroked the bad foot gently – and now the child can walk!"

"He does miracles! He is so good that he can do wonders. He is truly the son of God."

"Wherever he goes he comforts and heals and brings happiness. His eyes shine with goodness. His hands are full of healing power. Twice have I seen him, and I have said I will never do a wrong thing again. I felt that I *must* be good when I heard him preaching."

"It is both soul and body he heals and makes well. Let us go and hear him today. We will take the children too, because he loves them so."

The disciples went about with Jesus, marveling at his great gifts of healing, listening to his wonderful stories, told in such simple words, helping him, and caring for him when he was tired.

And everywhere he went the people flocked round him, anxious even to touch just the hem of his robe.

"Goodness flows out of him!" they said. "Truly he is the son of God!"

# Chapter 12

### *The Man by the Pool*

There was once a young man who had fallen ill. He lay groaning on his mattress, longing to get better. But the time went on, and he grew worse.

"I will take you to the Pool of Bethesda," said a friend of his. "Maybe when the angel comes down to the water and ripples it, you will be able to get into the pool and be healed."

So the friend took the young man to the strange pool. They went through the sheep market at Jerusalem and came to a building called Bethesda or the House of Mercy.

The young man looked curiously at the strange pool. Around it were built five porches. Steps led steeply down to the silent water below.

"I do not like this place," he said, mournfully. "See the miserable people lying about on the steps! They all look so ill and unhappy."

"You look the same," said the man who had brought him there. "Now listen – it is said that every now and again an angel comes down and troubles the water. If you can get into the pool first, when that happens, you will feel better. So you must do as all these others are doing, and lie here on the steps and watch the water. Then, as soon as you see it wrinkling and rippling, you must quickly get into it."

"Will you stay and help me?" asked the young man. But his friend was gone. He had to work to do. The young man was left alone.

He lay there, watching the surface of the pool eagerly. Would it wrinkle? Could he get down to the water first, before anyone else? He looked round the steps that led down to the pool. There were so many other people lying there!

They were ill, or lame, or paralyzed. Some were blind. They were all waiting for the angel to come down to the water.

They did not know that no angel ever came. The pool was fed by a spring, and when this sometimes bubbled up strongly, it ruffled the surface of the water, and the pool then had healing powers. But the people thought it must be an angel disturbing the pool, and they longed to get into it as soon as that happened.

One day the water suddenly began to stir and wrinkle. A murmur came from the watching people.

"The angel comes! See, the water is ruffled!"

And then friends helped them down to the pool quickly. Those without friends to help them tried their best to get down the steep steps by themselves.

The young man never had a friend near to help him. He watched the rippling of the water many many times, as the spring bubbled up, and he tried frantically to get down to the pool, crying, with everyone else, "The angel is here! He is here!"

But never once did he get into the water first. Year after year went by, and still the man lay there, no longer young now. He was thin and pale, and he grew older and thinner as the years passed. He still watched the water, but he was weaker now, and he was afraid that he would never, never get into the pool first, and feel its healing powers on his poor, ill body.

One day Jesus heard of the pool. He heard of the crowds of suffering people who lay there, and he was sad.

"I will go there," he said. "There may be someone I can help."

He passed through the porches, looking down with pity on the ill, unhappy people. He came to the man who had now been there for thirty-eight years. He saw how patient and sad he looked, and he knew that he had suffered pain and fear. He was full of compassion for him.

Jesus bent down over him, and spoke to him in his clear, kind voice. "Do you want to be healed?" he said.

"Sir," said the man, looking up in surprise at the kindness in the eyes of the stranger above him, "Sir, I have done my best to be healed, but I have no friend to put me down the steps quickly, so that I may get first into the water. I am always last."

Jesus was still looking at the man, and he said a strange thing to him.

"Rise, take up your bed and walk!"

Now the man had not been able to walk for years. He had been lying helpless on his mattress for most of his life! But as he looked into Jesus' eyes he knew perfectly well that he could obey his command. So he stood up, picked up his mattress, and walked!

The man was so astonished at himself that he thought he must be in a dream. He was walking! He was healed! He was as strong and well as the people in the streets outside.

He walked a few steps more in wonder and delight. Then he turned to speak to the amazing man who had told him to get up and walk. But Jesus had gone. He had slipped away in the crowd, and the man could not find him.

So he went back home through the streets, carrying his mattress, hardly able to believe what had happened to him. Then he suddenly noticed that people were looking at him very angrily. He wondered why.

"Oh, of course – it is the Sabbath day, when no one must work," remembered the man. "Carrying a bed is counted as work, and so the people are angry with me for breaking the law!"

Some Jews spoke sternly to him. "Why do you break the law by carrying your bed on the Sabbath day?"

The man poured out the whole story. "How can I help it? The man I speak of commanded me to rise up and walk, and I did! I do not know who he is. He is wonderful. You should have seen the goodness that shone from his eyes!"

The Jews did not care about Jesus' goodness. They were angry because he had told the man to carry his bed on the Sabbath day.

Now when the man went to the Temple that day to thank God for his new happiness, he saw Jesus there. He went to him at once in delight.

Jesus looked at him. "You are healed," he said. "Go, and do no more wrong in case a worse thing happens to you."

The man was so excited at seeing Jesus again that he ran to tell the Jews who had been angry with him. "There goes the man who healed me!" he said.

These Jews were jealous of Jesus because so many

people loved him and followed him. They sent for him and spoke angrily. "You know that it is against the law to work on the Sabbath day," they said.

"God, my father, does kind deeds on the Sabbath," said Jesus. "And so also do I!"

# Chapter 13

*The Poor Leper*

Aman went crying from his house. He left behind him his family and all his friends. He must never, never go near them again.

He was a leper. He had caught the terrible disease of leprosy, which ate his body away, and could never be cured. He must not go near anyone again, because if he touched them, they too might get the horrible disease.

"My wife! My children!" wept the poor man. "I must never see them again. I must go out alone in the countryside, and live with the other poor lepers. I must live as a beggar."

So he left his home and family, and went to live with the other lepers, lonely and afraid. No one cared for them, no one went near. If ever a stranger came by, the leper called out mournfully, "Unclean! Unclean!"

Then the stranger would shiver and hurry away in disgust. He had been near a leper. How terrible!

The poor man was very unhappy. He looked at the white leprosy spots on his body, and hated them. He wanted to be back with his family. He wanted to do his work once more, he wanted to talk and laugh with his friends. But he could never do those things again.

Now one day the leper saw a great crowd in the distance. He wondered what it was and suddenly a thought came into his mind.

He had heard of Jesus, the great healer. Could the crowd have come to be with Jesus? Was that why there were so many people gathered together in excitement? He dared not go near to find out because he was a leper and must never go near anyone.

He waited till the crowd had gone, then he went to where they had stood. Jesus was there. He had been preaching to the people, and healing many of them. The leper gazed at him, and knew at once that this man with the pitying eyes and beautiful face could be no one else but Jesus.

The leper knew that Jesus could heal him. He must tell him that he could heal him, if only he would! He went near Jesus and knelt down.

"Sir," he said, in a beseeching voice, "you can make me well if only you will!"

Jesus looked down. He saw the poor wretched leper, ugly and marked with leprosy. He did

what no one else in the world would have done. He
touched him with his hand.

"I will heal you," he said, in the clear voice that people
knew so well. "You are well again."

The leper looked down at himself when he heard these
marvelous words. He saw his sores healing up. He
watched his skin grow clean and whole again. He pulled
at his rags to see if his whole body was healed. Yes, it was.

"I am no longer a leper!" said the man, crying for joy.
"I am healed. See, my body is as it was when I was a
young man. I am healed! I am no longer unclean!"

Jesus saw the man's happiness, and he was glad. He
heard the words that tumbled out of the man's mouth.

"Sir! I can go back to my wife! I can love my children
again! I can seek out my friends. I can work and be
happy! This is a most wonderful thing you have done!"

Jesus saw that it was so very wonderful to the man
that he would most certainly go back at once to his
family, and tell his whole town of the miracle that had
happened to him.

Jesus did not want him to spread the news abroad so
that people would come flocking to him in their thousands to see what wonders he might do. It was difficult
to preach when so many hundreds pressed closer and
closer to him.

"See that you do not tell your news to everyone!"
Jesus said to the happy man. "Go to the priest and show

him that you are healed, and then go to your home. Do not tell everyone you meet what has happened."

But the man was so happy and so full of wonder that he could not help telling everyone he met.

"Don't shrink away from me!" he shouted. "I'm not a leper any more. I'm cured. Look, my skin is whole again. Jesus touched me and healed me. I'm just going to the priest."

The news went round at once. "The leper is healed! He says Jesus touched him and cured him. He is going back to his family. Did you ever hear of such a wonderful thing?"

The man quite forgot that Jesus had asked him not to spread his news abroad. He told his story over and over again to anyone who would hear him.

"We must go and see this marvelous man!" said everyone, and they flocked round Jesus in such crowds that it was quite impossible for him to preach to the people of that town.

"We will go into the quiet countryside," he said to his disciples, and they left this town and went out into the hills.

But the people came to him even there, and everywhere there was talk of Jesus.

"We must go and see this man Jesus! He is wonderful. Let us go to hear him. Come, we will go today, and take the children too, because he loves them."

# Chapter 14

*The Man Who Came Down Through the Roof*

Now, in the city of Capernaum there was a man who was so sick with the palsy that he could not move. He lay on his bed all day long, miserable and worried because he was of no use to himself or to anyone else.

He was grateful to the kind friends that came to see him. They told him the news each day, and brought him little gifts.

The man lay on his bed, unable to do anything but think. He puzzled about his terrible illness.

"Why has God struck me down in this dreadful way?" he wondered. "Is it a punishment for the wrong things I have done? I am sorry for them now. If only I could have my life over again! I would do as many good deeds as once I did wrong ones. Will God forgive me for all the sins I did? Does he know that I am sorry and ashamed now?"

One day his friends came in to see him as usual to tell him the news that was going round the city.

"There is news today!" said one friend. "We have heard of a man called Jesus who is a wonderful preacher

– and besides that, he can heal sick people."

"Yes! He has actually healed a leper!" said another man. "Such a thing has never been known before! Why, all lepers are incurable! And then Jesus touched this man, and he was healed. It's marvelous."

"Oh, he's done more wonderful things than that!" said another friend. "He cured a man who had been lying by the Pool of Bethesda for thirty-eight years. Think of that – thirty-eight years – and then Jesus came along and healed him."

The man with the palsy lay and listened, his eyes on his friends' excited faces. What a story this was to hear!

"It's a pity Jesus couldn't cure *you*," said one of the friends. "I wish he could."

"Tell me more about this man Jesus," begged the sick man. "Is he really good? What kind of things does he preach?"

"Oh, he is *really* good," said the friend. "He is always preaching that we should be kind to one another. He says, too, that our sins will be forgiven if we are sorry and really do try to do better."

The sick man lay and thought about this. He was so worried about the wrong things he had done in his life. "I have been unjust and unkind and ungenerous," he thought. "I wish I could see this man Jesus and ask him if he thinks God has forgiven me for my wrongdoing. I should feel happier then."

Not long after that, the man's friends came hurrying into his house, looking excited and pleased.

"Jesus is here! In Capernaum itself! We met somebody who told us so."

"He's gone to a house not very far off," said one of the men. "You should see the crowds! And I heard that very learnèd men, who know the law from beginning to end, are actually going to hear him speak today. We're going to see him."

"We'll tell you all about it when we come back," said another friend.

The sick man looked up at them. How he longed to go with them! How he wished he too could walk to where Jesus was and listen to him! But he couldn't.

"We'll take you with us!" said one friend suddenly. "There are four of us. We will each take a corner of your mattress, and carry you like that!"

So they did as they said, and each took a mattress corner. Then, with the sick man between them, they went to find Jesus.

Jesus was already in one of the houses. It was one of many that were built around a big courtyard. Already there were hundreds upon hundreds of people there, pressing into the courtyard, pushing through the gateway, talking excitedly, all anxious for a glimpse of the wonderful preacher.

The four men with the sick man on his bed could not

possibly get through the crowds. They set the bed down in despair.

"We can't push through all these people," said one. "We'd better go home again."

The sick man was bitterly disappointed. He looked so despairing that the friends felt as if they must do something. But what could they do?

"I've thought of a plan," said one at last. "Let's go up the outside stairs of the house, and get up on to the flat roof. We'll dig a hole in the roof, and let our friend down carefully into the room below."

"Jesus won't be angry," said another man. "They say he is goodness itself."

The four friends took the man on his mattress up the steps to the flat roof of the house. Most of these flat roofs were made of hard earth, so it would not be very difficult to dig a hole in this one, if it too was of earth.

"Yes – it is made of hard earth," said one man, and he began to scrape at the roof. The sick man lay nearby and watched eagerly. This was like a dream! Would he really be able to see Jesus?

The four men dug hard at the roof. They made a hole, and they put in their hands and began to break away big pieces. Soon there was a space big enough to let down the man on his bed.

The people in the room below were most astonished. What could be happening? First there was the sound of

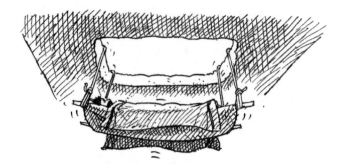

digging, then a hole appeared, and then bits and pieces began to drop down into the room below.

"Look – what's this coming down now?" said someone in alarm. It was the bed swinging down on ropes through the hole with the sick man lying on it. The friends watched anxiously as they lowered the man care-

fully to the floor below. Then, when he was safely there, they peered through the hole, wondering what would happen to their friend.

The sick man lay on his bed at the feet of Jesus. He looked up at him. He saw at once that Jesus was wise and good. He could help him. He could tell him if his sins were forgiven him, and could teach him how to be good.

Jesus was surprised at the sudden appearance of the man on the bed. He was touched at the way the four men had helped their friend, and trusted him to help the poor man too.

Everyone in the room was watching, hardly daring to breathe. Would there be another miracle?

Jesus looked down at the man. He knew at once what it was that he wanted more than anything else.

"Man," Jesus said, in his grave, clear voice, "your sins are forgiven you."

The man sighed with happiness. That was what he wanted to hear, what he had come to ask. He was glad and very grateful.

But there were others there who were not glad to hear these words. The learnèd men sat and frowned.

"How dare this man tell the fellow his sins are forgiven him?" they thought. "Only God can forgive sins."

Jesus looked round at them. He read their hard thoughts at once.

"What are you thinking?" he asked. "Tell me, which do you think it is easier to say to a man like this: 'Your sins are forgiven you,' or 'Rise up and walk'? You shall see that I have power to forgive sins, although you think me an ordinary man."

He looked at the man on the bed. "Arise, take up your bed and go to your house," he commanded.

The sick man heard. His eyes shone. He arose, stood steadily on his feet, picked up his bed, and walked!

"See! He who has not walked for years is healed," whispered the people to one another. "He has risen, taken his bed, and walked home, as he was bidden. And his sins are forgiven him!"

The four men scrambled off the roof to join their happy friend.

"We have seen strange and wonderful things," they said in awe. "Truly this man is the son of God!"

# Chapter 15

*The Soldier and his Servant*

There was once an officer who lived in Capernaum, and commanded a company of Herod's soldiers there.

He was not a Jew, but he liked Jews and was good to them.

"I will build you a new church in Capernaum," he told them. "It shall be a fine church, as fine as I can make it."

Now one day his favorite servant fell very ill. He was more like a friend than a servant, and the soldier was grieved when he heard that the doctors could not cure him.

Like everyone else in Capernaum, the officer had heard of Jesus and all his wonderful teachings and miracles.

"I wonder if he could help me," he thought. "No, I cannot ask him, for I am not a Jew. It is the Jews he helps and preaches to. But perhaps if I send to the chief men of the Jewish church I built, *they* might ask Jesus for me. They could tell him about my beloved servant."

So he sent a message to the chief men of the church and asked them if they would go to Jesus for him.

They went at once to find Jesus. They were proud that such a rich and important man wanted Jesus.

"We will tell him how this officer built us our fine church, and what a very important man he is," they said to one another.

But Jesus did not listen to all their talk of how rich and important the officer was. He heard only two things: that a soldier loved his servant very much, and that he was grieved because the man was ill. Those were the two things that mattered to Jesus.

He set off at once to the soldier's house. But the officer had changed his mind now.

"How can I possibly bother such a great and good man to come all the way to my house?" he thought. "He has only to say the word, and my servant would be better at once, without even being seen by Jesus! I am troubling him for nothing. I will send my friends to Jesus and ask him merely to say the

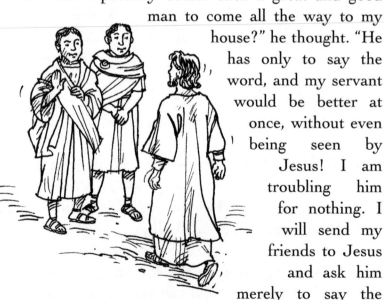

word, and my servant will be better. He must not trouble himself to come to my house."

So on the way there Jesus was stopped by a few men, sent by the officer.

"Lord, do not trouble yourself to come further on your way," they said. "Our friend has told us to come to you and say that he is not worthy for you to come into his house, neither is he worthy to come to you himself."

Jesus listened in surprise. The soldier's friends gave him the rest of the message.

"Lord, he asks you simply to say the word and he is certain that his servant will be healed. Does he not say to his soldiers 'Go!' and they go, 'Come!' and they come, and to his servant 'Do this and do that!'? You, Lord, can do the same, and your word too will be obeyed. Say the word, and our friend's servant will at once be healed."

Jesus was astonished and very pleased. He spoke to the people who were with him.

"No one has ever put such trust in me before, not even my own people!"

He turned to the soldier's friends. "So shall it be. The servant shall be healed!"

The friends hurried back to the house, and there the soldier met them. His eyes shone with joy.

"You gave Jesus my message!" he said. "And I know he said the word. My servant is healed. He is well again. Come and see!"

# Chapter 16

*Jesus in the Storm*

One evening, after Jesus had been telling the people many many stories, he was tired.

"Master, you must rest," said Peter. "Leave the people now and rest yourself."

Jesus had been sitting in the boat, talking from there to the people. They could not press against him if he sat a little way out on the water, and they could hear his voice clearly, and see him as he talked.

Jesus looked at the crowds on the shore. "If we land there, the people will follow us, and we shall get no rest," he said. "Let us take the boat to the other side of the lake. When the people see us sailing away they will all go home."

So Peter headed the little fishing-boat out on the open water. Jesus lay down. He was very tired indeed. He could not keep his eyes open. He rested his head on a cushion and fell fast asleep.

The boat moved over the water, and the waves splashed against the sides. The boat bobbed a little, but Jesus slept on.

"Do not wake him," said Peter, in a low voice. "He

is so tired."

So they let the boat sail on gently, and watched the sleeping Jesus. But suddenly Peter grew anxious.

"Look!" he said. "See that great black cloud coming up! And feel the wind – it's blowing up more and more strongly."

"It's one of the storms that blow up so quickly on our lake," said another disciple. "We should not be so far out, Peter! See how high the waves are rising. Our boat will be overturned."

"It's getting dark too," said Peter, even more anxious. "Why did we come out so far? Hark at the wind! It is howling already – and that big black cloud has completely covered the sky."

The boat began to rock dangerously. To and fro it went, tipping over almost to the water. The waves rose very high, and spray blew over the disciples, and over the sleeping Jesus.

"He must be very very tired not to wake with all this wind and tossing about," said Peter. "And see – a wave splashed over him then and he did not move. The boat will soon be full of water!"

The disciples trembled with fear as the boat rocked more and more, filling with water from the waves that splashed over the side. "Wake Jesus," they said to Peter. "Do you want us to be drowned?"

Peter bent over Jesus. He shook him by the shoulder

and shouted in his ear above the sound of the wind and the waves. "Master, awake! Master, save us!"

Jesus awoke suddenly. He sat up and saw how dark it was, and heard how the wind howled. Spray whipped against his face, and the boat rocked badly.

He stood up in the rocking boat, and the disciples heard his clear, commanding voice.

"Peace, be still!" Jesus said to the wind and the waves. Then the wind dropped at once and ceased its howling, and the waves died down so that the boat no

longer rocked. A great calm came over the lake.

The disciples watched in the greatest awe. Jesus turned to them.

"Why are you so frightened?" he said. "Do you not trust me even yet?"

The disciples said nothing. They gazed at their master, filled with wonder, marveling at this man who had suddenly calmed the storm.

"What manner of man is this?" they said to one another. "Even the wind and the waves obey him!"

# Chapter 17

*The Poor Madman*

The disciples spent the night in the boat with Jesus. When morning dawned, it was a lovely day.

"Sail over to the other side of the lake," said Jesus. "I must rest and pray."

So the boat sailed away, and came to the other side of the lake to the place where the Gadarenes lived.

"We will go up into the hills," said Jesus when they had moored the boat, and they climbed up the lonely hillside, talking together.

And then a very frightening thing happened. Out of a cave rushed a dreadful man, shouting and yelling, shaking his fist in rage. He wore no clothes, he had let his hair and beard grow long, and he looked very fierce indeed.

He was a poor madman that everyone was afraid of. He was very strong and very fierce, and even when he had been tied with ropes and chains he had broken them and got loose again. He was as strong as a giant when he was in one of his rages.

He lived in a horrible cave, and lay in wait for people

to come by. Then he would rush out at them and terrify them. He was a mad, bad, unhappy man, hated and feared by everyone.

He rushed out at the disciples, yelling and howling. All at once he caught sight of Jesus. He stopped shouting and gazed at him. He had never seen a man look pityingly and kindly at him before. He rushed to Jesus, and the disciples moved closer in case he should try to hurt their master.

But the madman fell at his feet and tried to take hold of his ankles. The disciples moved away in disgust. What a horrible fellow – and how dangerous!

Jesus did not move away. He looked down with great compassion in his eyes. Poor, muddled madman, troubled and unhappy! Jesus was not disgusted or afraid. He looked into the wild face of the madman and spoke to him in the voice that made everyone listen.

"What is your name?" he said.

"My name!" cried the man wildly. "I have a thousand names, for there are a thousand bad devils inside me, they make me do bad things, they make me wicked! I have as many names as I have devils in me!"

"Then I will take away those thousand devils," said Jesus, calmly, and his voice quietened the wild, excited man. "They shall all leave you, and you shall find yourself again."

The madman listened, his eyes on the grave, steady face above him. He saw love and pity and wise understanding there, things he had not seen for years. His wild, unhappy soul drank in the love and pity. He suddenly grew quiet and stopped shaking. His mind cleared and he could think again, clearly and sensibly. His madness left him – he was himself again!

The man stood up. He gazed at Jesus with the greatest love and devotion. Who was this wonderful man who had done this to him? How he worshiped him! He seemed like God himself to the hairy, ugly man from the caves.

He looked down at himself and was horrified to see

that he was so dirty and had no clothes on.

"Take my cloak," said one of the disciples, kindly, and the man wrapped himself in it.

He would not leave Jesus. He sat at his feet all day long, listening to him. Someone had cared enough to be kind to him, someone had had enough love to make him better! The poor man could hardly believe it.

"I will never leave you," he said to Jesus.

But Jesus shook his head and said, "If you really love me and want to do something for me, stay here with your own people and tell them what has happened to you. Tell them what you have heard me say. Then if I come here again I shall find the people ready to listen to me."

And so the man stayed behind when Jesus sailed away in the boat, sad to see him go, but glad that he could do something, however small, to show how much he loved the man who had healed him of his madness.

# Chapter 18

*A Blind Man Is Made Happy*

There was once a blind man called Bartimaeus. Each day he made his way stumblingly to the roadside, and sat there, hoping for a little kindness from the passers-by.

He sat on the road near the big town of Jericho. Many beggars sat there with him, because so many people passed in and out of Jericho, and always there were a few who threw coins or bread to the poor beggars.

Bartimaeus had his place with the others. He envied them because they could see and he could not. He could only hear the footsteps of the passers-by, he could not see the people going to and fro. He lived in a world of darkness.

When he heard footsteps, he would call out loudly: "Have pity on a poor blind beggar! Have pity, and spare a little money for one who cannot work! Have pity on one who lives in darkness and cannot see the light!"

Some passers-by were fully of pity for the blind man and pressed a coin into his outstretched hand. They knew he could not work, so they helped him a little.

Now one day Bartimaeus was sitting by the roadside as usual when he thought he heard more footsteps than he had ever heard before.

"There must be quite a crowd of people hurrying by!" he thought. "Why, there must be hundreds of people this morning. Where are they going?"

He listened again. "Yes, there are crowds of people about today. How I wish I could see them! What is the matter, I wonder? Why are there so many?"

At last Bartimaeus felt that he really must find out what all the excitement was about. So he called out loudly.

"Won't somebody tell me what is going on! I'm blind, I can't see. What is the excitement about? Why are there so many people this morning?"

"Oh, haven't you heard?" answered someone. "It's Jesus of Nazareth! He's passing here this morning and we're all watching for him. He'll soon be here."

"Jesus of Nazareth!" said Bartimaeus. "Think of that! He's the great healer, the one who makes sick people better. He's coming by here – where I'm sitting! If only he would see me! Jesus of Nazareth, they said. It's too good to be true."

He heard more and more footsteps. He heard the excited cries of the crowds. He heard what they said.

"Jesus has come! Look, there he is, walking with his friends."

Bartimaeus listened. Jesus must be very near. If only he could *see* – but he was blind, he could see nothing.

Bartimaeus could keep silent no longer. He raised his voice and shouted. He shouted more loudly than he had ever shouted before: "Jesus, have pity on me! Jesus, have pity on me!"

"Bartimaeus, be quiet," said the people. "How can you make such a terrible noise?"

Bartimaeus took no notice. He went on shouting:
"JESUS, HAVE PITY ON ME!"

Everyone nearby was angry to think that a blind beggar should make such a noise. They shouted at him, ordering him to be quiet.

"JESUS, HAVE PITY ON ME!" called Bartimaeus again and again.

Jesus heard the loud, urgent voice. He stopped at once. He saw the blind man sitting by the wayside.

"Bring him here to me," said Jesus. The people ran to Bartimaeus at once.

"Get up, fellow! Jesus has sent for you," they told him.

Bartimaeus trembled for joy. He stood up and stretched out his hands to feel his way to Jesus. He was guided right up to him.

Jesus looked at the blind man with compassion. "What do you want of me?" He asked gently.

"Lord, if only I could see!" said Bartimaeus.

Jesus put out his hand and touched the man's blind eyes. Bartimaeus stood still, hardly believing what had happened to him.

He could see! The darkness had fled. He was in the golden sunshine. He could see colors and light. And he could see the beautiful face of the man who had taken him out of his darkness. He could see Jesus of Nazareth!

He shouted and sang for joy. He leapt about and cried out his happiness. He could not believe his good fortune. Jesus of Nazareth had come by! Jesus of Nazareth had stopped for him!

He followed Jesus all day long, telling the crowds of the miracle. They were glad for him and rejoiced with him.

But the happiest of all was Bartimaeus himself.

# Chapter 19

*The Little Daughter of Jairus*

A little girl was watching for her father to come home. She lived at Capernaum, the town where Jesus often came.

"Where are you, Anna?" called her mother. The dark-eyed, dark-haired child called back: "I am waiting for my father. He will play with me when he comes."

Anna was twelve years old, an only child, and her parents loved her with all their hearts. She went everywhere with them, and they were very proud of her.

Each day when Jairus, her father, came home they played a game together. Anna always looked forward to that. Now she was watching for him as usual.

"Here he is!" she cried, and ran to meet the big man whose eyes and hair were so like hers. They played their game and the mother heard them laughing and talking happily in the evening sunshine. She smiled happily too.

But none of them smiled the next day. Anna fell ill. "My head is hot," she said. "It hurts. I don't want anything to eat. I don't want to play."

Her father was suddenly anxious. "Wife, the child looks really ill," he said. "Put her to bed. I will send for the doctor."

So Anna was put to bed. She tossed restlessly from side to side. The doctor came and left her some medicine.

"She is no better," said the mother that evening. "I am afraid she is worse. We will send for the doctor again."

The doctor was alarmed when he came. "I will get another doctor," he said. "The child is very ill. Perhaps a second doctor can help."

But in a day or two it was plain that Anna was desperately ill. Her father was in despair.

"She is my only child," he kept thinking, "my dear beloved little Anna. What can I do for her? The doctor has given her up. He can do nothing. I cannot let her die!"

He sat by the child's bedside and watched her. He looked at his anxious wife; she was pale and sad.

"Have you heard of this new healer, the man called Jesus?" he said suddenly. "I've been thinking about him. I think he is here, in the town."

"Go and fetch him," said his wife at once. "He might come and lay his hand on our child and make her well. Go now, Jairus, before it is too late."

"I will go and ask where I can find him," said Jairus. "He is a good man and he loves little children. Surely he would come to our little Anna."

Jairus stroked his little girl's hair and went quietly out

of the room. He made his way into the town and asked people anxiously where he could find Jesus. He went to the house where Jesus stayed – but alas, he was not here!

"Go down to the lakeside," said the woman who opened the door to him. "He may be preaching there."

So Jairus went down to the blue water, and there he saw a great crowd of people. "Surely Jesus must be here," he thought gladly.

He pressed through the crowd. "Is Jesus here?" he asked. "Where is he?"

"No, he is not here," said someone. "He was with us only last night, telling us stories from Peter's boat. Then he sailed off over the lake. A storm blew up when it was dark and we hope Jesus is safe. We are waiting for the boat to come back."

"Will he be long?" said Jairus, in despair. Nobody knew.

"You can only wait," said a woman nearby, sorry for this man who looked so worried. So Jairus stood with the people and waited, straining his eyes to see across the lake. He thought of Anna, lying so ill. Was she still alive? Every minute mattered now. If only Jesus would come!

"There's a boat now," said somebody, and Jairus sighed with relief. But it was not Peter's boat. It was someone else's. Jairus's heart sank.

After a little while somebody shouted: "I can see the boat. Look, over there! Jesus is coming!"

Peter's boat sailed swiftly over the lake. Jairus could see a man standing in it. Yes, it was Jesus himself. The boat ran into shore, and willing hands helped to pull it in. Jesus sprang to the beach, and the disciples tried to keep back the people crowding round him.

Jesus did not land near Jairus, who had to push through the crowd. "Let me through," he begged everyone. "Do let me through."

The crowd opened to let him pass. They saw that he had something urgent to say to Jesus. Jairus knelt down in front of Jesus and begged him to come and see his little girl.

"She is at the point of death," said Jairus, his voice trembling. "I pray you, Lord, come and put your hands on her that she may be healed. Then she will live."

Jesus saw that Jairus was desperate. "I will come at once," he said. "Let us go."

Everyone had been listening to what Jairus had said. "He's going to see the little girl," they said to one another. "Little Anna, you know. He'll do something wonderful! We must go and see."

The crowd jostled and pressed round Jesus and the disciples as they went with Jairus. They were excited, and every moment more and more people came to join them.

Now, in the crowd, there was a poor, miserable woman. She was ill with a disease that no doctor seemed able to cure. For twelve years she had spent all her money on doctors, and now she was worse.

She had heard of Jesus, of course. "I would never dare to speak to him, or ask him to heal me," she thought. "But suppose, in the crowd, I got near enough just to touch the hem of his robe or even the tassel on his cloak – why, that would be enough to make me well again. He is so good and so kind – yes, just to touch his cloak would heal me!"

So, as Jesus was walking along with the Jairus, this woman made her way nearer and nearer to him in the crowd. At last she was just behind him. With a beating heart she put out her hand and touched the bottom of his cloak.

No sooner had she touched it than she felt herself healed! Her body felt different. It was suddenly strong and healthy. The woman was overcome with joy and wonder. Now she must get away quickly and think of the marvelous thing that had happened to her.

But before she could go, Jesus stopped and looked round. "Who touched me?" he said.

"I didn't, master," said one nearby. "Nor did I," said another. Peter was astonished at his master's question.

"Master, what do you mean, *who touched you*?" said he. "Look at the crowd round you, jostling against you all the time! Many people must have touched you."

But Jesus knew quite well that someone had touched him on purpose, because he had felt goodness going out of him as always happened when he healed someone. Some person had wanted his help, and had got it without even asking for it. Who was it?

Jairus did not want to stop. "Oh, hurry, hurry!" he thought. "There is so little time to be lost."

The woman in the crowd felt that Jesus was looking at her. She came forward and knelt down, trembling. She told him of the disease she had had.

"I knew that if I touched but the hem of your cloak I should be healed," she said. "And it was so."

"Daughter," said Jesus, gently, "because you trusted me so much, you were healed. Go in peace."

# Chapter 20

*Jesus Saves Anna*

As the woman was slipping through the crowd Jairus suddenly saw messengers pushing their way through the people. "Where is Jairus?" they asked. "We want Jairus."

Jairus felt his heart go cold, for the faces of the messengers were grave and sad. "Sir," said one, "do not trouble the master now. Your little girl is dead."

Jairus turned in despair to Jesus, tears in his eyes. It was too late after all!

Jesus spoke comfortingly to him. "Don't be afraid. Only believe in me."

He walked on with Jairus, and the crowd followed. When he came near the house Jesus turned and spoke to the people.

"Come no further," he said. Then, taking James and Peter and John with him, he went into the house with Jairus.

As soon as they were inside they heard a great noise of weeping and wailing and doleful singing and chanting. In those days when anyone died people were paid to come and wail for the dead, and already they were wailing for little Anna.

Jesus could not bear this noise. He knew that the people there had been paid to weep and wail, they were not weeping from their hearts for Anna. It was all make-believe, and Jesus did not like that.

"Why do you make this noise?" Jesus said to the weeping women. "The little girl is not dead. She is asleep."

Then they all laughed at him, for they had seen that the child was dead. Jesus sent them all away, and then he followed Jairus into the room where Anna lay. His disciples went with him, and they walked softly to the bed where the child lay so still.

The mother was there, weeping bitterly. "You were too late, Jairus," she sobbed. "You did not even say goodbye to her, our poor little Anna."

Jairus looked at her in despair, and then turned to Jesus. No one but Jesus could do anything now.

Jesus stood by the bed, looking at the child who lay so still, her eyes closed, and her cheeks pale.

He put out his hand and took Anna's in his. He held it firmly in his warm one.

"Get up, little one," he said.

Anna opened her eyes. She sat up, looking all round. She was surprised to see so many men round her bed. She smiled at her father. Then she got up from her bed and walked a few steps in the room.

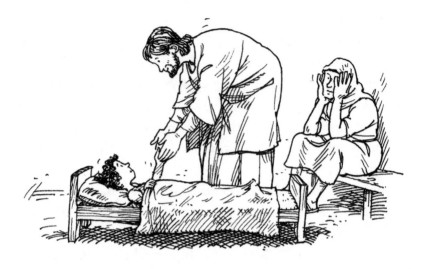

Her mother and father could hardly believe their eyes. "Anna!" said her mother. "My little Anna!"

And in a moment she was in the arms of her father and mother. They kissed her and hugged her, crying for joy. She was alive again! She was laughing and talking just as usual!

Jesus watched them with gladness. It was always good to see love and happiness and he was glad that he could bring so much.

"Tell no one of this," he said to Jairus. Then he turned to Anna's mother. She was quite beside herself with joy. Jesus knew that he must give her something to do for her child.

"Give Anna something to eat," he said, and the mother

went gladly to fetch some good.

Jesus went from the house with his disciples, leaving behind a very happy family.

"I want to see that man again," said Anna, to her parents. "He is kind. I like him."

And so, when Jesus visited Capernaum, and the children came round him as they always did, little Anna was always there, waiting. She listened to his stories, gazing up into his clear, steadfast eyes. She would do anything in the world for Jesus!

# Chapter 21

*Judas the Traitor*

J udas was one of the disciples of Jesus. He was clever, and the others trusted him to do many things for them.

"You can go and bargain in the town for the food we need," they said to Judas. "We have very little money and you can make the best of what we have. You are good at dealing with money and keeping account of it."

Judas was a strange man. Although he was one of the disciples, he did not love Jesus. The only person he really loved was himself.

At first he had believed in Jesus, and thought he was a very wonderful man, so powerful that it would not be long before he became a king.

"And when he is king he will remember all his disciples and friends," thought the cunning Judas, "and I shall be among them. I shall become a prince, at least! I shall have much power and a great deal of money."

The months went by and Judas found that Jesus was certainly not going to be the kind of king that Judas imagined. And what was this kingdom that Jesus so often spoke of? Why, it was only a kingdom of love! It wasn't a real kingdom with palaces and soldiers and courtiers and plenty of money flowing in – it was simply a kingdom of love, to which the poorest of the land could belong.

Judas was scornful of such a kingdom. He had not given up his work to follow Jesus for that!

"This man is full of a strange power. He can work the most wonderful miracles," thought Judas. "Then why does he not work miracles for himself and for us? He could so easily make us rich and strong and powerful! But he doesn't. He simply goes round talking and preaching, and healing the sick. I wish I had never followed him!"

The traitor said nothing to the others of what he thought. Then one day he became afraid. Some of the powerful men of Jerusalem, the Chief Priests, the Scribes and the Pharisees, were making threats against Jesus. They were angry because the poor people loved him, followed him and believed every word he said. They were jealous and bitter.

Judas knew this. He knew that if the Chief Priests could take Jesus and throw him into prison with his disciples, they would be glad.

"I don't want to go to prison," thought Judas. "I must look after myself. I will go to the Chief Priests and tell them I will help them to capture Jesus, if they will pay me. Then I shall be safe."

Now it happened that Caiaphas, the High Priest, was calling a meeting of the rulers of Jerusalem to decide how they could take Jesus and put him into prison.

"We will capture him as soon as we can," said Caiaphas. "But not just yet. There is a great festival in Jerusalem this week, and the town is full of people who love Jesus. We will wait till the week is over, then we will see what we can do to take this man."

Someone came into the room where they were holding their meeting, someone who made the priests stare in amazement.

It was Judas – Judas, one of the very disciples of the man they had been talking of. What did he want?

He soon told them. "I will help you to capture Jesus," said Judas. "How much will you give me if I do?"

This made things very easy for the priests. They were delighted. "We will give you thirty pieces of silver!" said Caiaphas. "That is the price of a slave, and is good for you."

"Pay me now," said Judas. He did not trust anyone because he was untrustworthy himself. The priests counted out thirty pieces of silver for the traitor.

"I will send you word when you can capture Jesus," said Judas. "I will choose a time when there are few people about to interfere."

Then he left the meeting with the money in his bag – and with a terrible secret in his heart. "Nobody guesses what I have done," he thought. "I have sold Jesus for thirty pieces of silver. I am rich!"

But Jesus knew what he had done, and he was grieved and sad at heart.

# Chapter 22

*The Last Supper*

It was festival week in Jerusalem. The sacred Feast of the Passover was being held. Jesus wanted to eat the feast for the last time with his disciples, before he was betrayed by Judas.

"Go and prepare the feast in a room I will tell you of," said Jesus to Peter and John. So the two disciples went to the room that a friend had lent to Jesus for the feast, and got it ready.

Round the table were drawn couches, for in those long-ago days people lay on couches to eat their meals and did not sit on chairs. The feast was of bread made without yeast, roast lamb, a sauce, a bitter salad, and wine to drink. Peter and John prepared everything ready for the meal.

Some of the disciples wanted to take the chief seats at the table. Jesus saw this. Had they still not learned that such things did not matter? How could he show them that it was wrong and foolish always to try and get the best seats, the finest food, the most attention?

Now usually at a feast there was a servant who welcomed the guests, and brought water to wash their dirty, dusty feet. But there was no servant that night.

"I will be their servant," thought Jesus. "I will show them that although I am called master by them all, I am their humble and loving servant too, as we all should be to one another."

Jesus took off his long cloak and wide belt, and tied a towel round his waist. He took water and poured it into a basin on the floor. And then he went from one disciple to another, washing and wiping their feet.

The disciples were astonished. Peter tried to stop Jesus from washing his feet – but when Jesus said, "He that would be chief among you shall be servant of all," he and the others knew what Jesus meant, and they were silent.

The great feast began. Jesus broke the bread and blessed it, and then gave it to his disciples. He said to them, "Take ye and eat. This is my body."

He handed them the cup of wine and said, "Drink ye all of this. For this is my blood, which shall be shed for many."

Then he told the disciples that he was soon to die, but that he would come again to them before he went up to his father in heaven.

And still we keep this feast ourselves and call it the Holy Communion, eating bread, drinking wine, and remembering how Jesus gave his body and his blood for all of us who welcome his kingdom of love. It is our Feast of Remembrance, our way of coming close to the Lord and master.

# Chapter 23

## *In the Garden of Gethsemane*

When Jesus and his disciples had finished their supper – the last one that Jesus had with them – Judas slipped away.

The time had come for him to betray Jesus. It was dark. Judas knew that soon Jesus was going into the lonely Garden of Gethsemane with his disciples. It would be a good time for the priests to come and take him.

Jesus waited until Judas had gone. Then he gave his disciples a new commandment – the very greatest and most important of all his commandments.

"I give you a new commandment," he said. "Love one another."

He did not give it only to his disciples. He gave it to us as well. It is a commandment we should never forget.

Then Jesus arose and took his disciples to the quiet Garden of Gethsemane. He left all but Peter, James, and John at the gate. He wanted these three near him, because he was very sad.

He knew that his work on earth was finished, and that soon some very terrible things would happen to him.

Judas had gone to betray him. Jesus needed to pray and to get courage and comfort from his heavenly father. Although he was the son of God he was also the son of man, and he felt the same things that we feel, and suffered pain and unhappiness just as we do.

"Wait here and keep awake," he said to the three disciples, and he went a little way away to pray.

After a while he went back to his disciples, feeling lonely and unhappy. They were all asleep.

"Could you not keep awake for me one hour?" said Jesus, sadly, and once again he went to pray to God. He knew that in a very short time Judas would come with soldiers to take him.

Jesus went to his disciples twice more – and at the third time his face was full of courage.

"Rise!" he said. "Let us be gone. Our betrayer is here."

Judas had been to Caiaphus. "Go now to the Garden of Gethsemane," he said. "Jesus is there with his disciples. It will be easy to take him there, in the dark of night."

# Chapter 24

*The Capture of Jesus*

There came a noise at the gate, and in marched soldiers, priests, servants, and the Temple Guard. They were armed with sticks and swords. They carried torches, and the flames lighted up the olive trees in the garden.

"Judas, how shall we know which man is Jesus?" asked the priests.

"I will go to him and kiss him," said Judas. "You must watch to see which man I greet, and seize him."

Judas went straight up to Jesus, who was standing silently beneath an olive tree.

"Hail, master!" said Judas, kissed him, as was his custom.

Jesus looked at him sadly and sternly. "Judas, do you betray me with a kiss?" he said. Then he turned to the crowd of excited men nearby.

"Whom do you seek?" he asked.

"Jesus of Nazareth," they answered.

"I am he," said Jesus.

Peter drew his sword, ready to defend Jesus to the death. He struck out at a man nearby.

"Peter, put away your sword," commanded Jesus. He turned to the crowd once more.

"Have you come against me as if I were a thief, with stick and swords? You laid no hand on me when I sat each day in the Temple, preaching. But now your time has come – this is your hour, and the powers of evil must have their way."

Then the soldiers laid hands on Jesus and took him. And all his disciples forsook him and fled.

# Chapter 25

*Before the Cock Crowed Twice*

Peter followed the soldiers and priests a good way behind. He was afraid. How terrible to see Jesus, so wonderful and so powerful in all he could do for others, being marched away like a common thief! Peter could not understand it.

Jesus had known that the bold, impulsive Peter would be afraid. At the Last Supper he had told him something that the disciple had not believed.

"Although you say you would follow me and go with me to imprisonment or death, Peter, I tell you that before the cock crows twice, you will three times deny that you know me," he had said.

Now Peter, trembling and amazed, was full of fear as he followed the little company to the house of Caiaphas, the High Priest. He managed to get into the big courtyard of the house, and he went to a fire to warm himself, for he was cold and miserable.

A maid servant was there, and she knew him. "You are one of that man's disciples, aren't you?" she said.

"Woman, I have never known Jesus," said Peter, loudly.

Somewhere a cock crowed, for it was almost day.

Then someone else called out to Peter, "You are one of the followers of Jesus."

"Man, I am not," said Peter at once.

And yet a third man said, "Surely this man is one of Jesus' friends – hear how he speaks! He comes from Galilee, like Jesus!"

"I tell you I do not know this man!" shouted Peter, angrily.

Then the cock crowed for the second time, and Peter suddenly remembered what Jesus had said. He had said that Peter would deny him three times before the cock crowed twice. And in spite of all the brave things he had said to his beloved master, Peter had been a coward, and had denied that he knew him.

Poor Peter! With a breaking heart he went out of the courtyard into the street, and wept bitterly.

# Chapter 26

*The Trial of Jesus*

Jesus was in prison, mocked at and scorned. His disciples had left him, and he was lonely and sad.

Caiaphas the High Priest had ordered him to be taken to the Roman governor, Pilate. Pilate would put Jesus to death! That was what the priests wanted – they must somehow get rid of this man whom the common people loved so much.

The Romans were rulers over the Jews. If only the Jews could think of bad things to say about Jesus, if they could say that he was planning to be a king, then Pilate would perhaps think Jesus meant to lead an army against the Roman rulers, and overthrow them to make himself king.

"After all, Jesus has said he is king," said the priests to one another. So he had – he had said that he was bringing them *his* kingdom of love.

"We will tell Pilate that this man sets himself up to be a king," they decided, and so, shouting and yelling, they went to the court with Jesus and told Pilate the things they had determined to say.

Jesus said nothing. The Jews shouted continually.

Pilate decided to take the prisoner into his palace and question him alone. So he ordered Jesus to be brought to him, and he questioned him closely.

He soon saw that there was no harm in this grave man with the steady eyes and clear voice. He would never lead any army against the Romans!

He went out to the Chief Priests.

"I find no fault in this man!" said Pilate, meaning to set Jesus free at once. But the crowd were so angry that Pilate hardly knew what to do.

Then he remembered that Jesus came from Galilee. Herod, the king ruled over Galilee, not Pilate. He could get rid of this man by sending him to the Jewish king, Herod. Herod was in Jerusalem every day. He could judge this man and do what he liked with him.

So Jesus was taken away to Herod. Herod had heard about him, and knew that he did many miracles. But Jesus did none for Herod. He stood there, silent, while everyone mocked him, Herod too.

"You think you're a king, do you?" said Herod. "Well, you shall be dressed as one. Fetch one of my red cloaks, and wrap it round this fellow!"

Then Herod sent Jesus back to Pilate, and dressed as a king so that everyone might see him and laugh at him.

Pilate did not want to harm Jesus, and he certainly did not want to kill him. He did not find any fault in him worthy of great punishment or of death. He thought that he would set Jesus free.

But the crowd would not let him. "Do not set him free! Set the robber Barabbas free instead!" they cried. "Crucify Jesus! Hang him on a cross and let him die!"

# Chapter 27

*Jesus on the Cross*

Pilate set the robber Barabbas free, and gave orders that Jesus was to be beaten. The soldiers were cruel and merciless to him.

"Does this fellow call himself King of the Jews?" they said. "Well, we will crown him and give him a scepter and a throne!"

So they gave Jesus a chair for a throne, and they made him a crown of thorns that pricked his head, and they put a stick in his hand for a scepter. They mocked at poor, tired Jesus and had no pity for him.

In the prison with Jesus there were two other prisoners. They were robbers, and they too were to hang on crosses with Jesus.

Each of the prisoners had to carry his own heavy cross. Jesus had his over his shoulder, and he could hardly drag the weight along, for he was tired and had been beaten by the soldiers. He fell down, and the soldiers had to take someone from the crowd to carry his cross for him.

The guards took the three men to a hill outside the city, called Golgotha. They fastened the men to their

crosses and let them hang there for all to see. People mocked at Jesus as he hung there in the hot sun, thirsty and in great pain.

"Ho! You have many a time saved others! But now you can't even save yourself!"

Some of Jesus' friends came there, and his mother Mary stood near, weeping bitterly. How could this happen to her good and noble son, at whose birth all the angels in heaven had sung?

Jesus was sad for his mother. He spoke to John, the disciple he loved most of all.

"Behold your mother!" he said. Then he spoke to his mother. "Behold your son!"

They both knew what he meant, and from that day John looked after Mary as if she were his own mother.

Jesus was a man like other men, and he had to bear the same pain as the two robbers bore, and to feel the same great fear and unhappiness. He felt almost as if God, his heavenly father, had forsaken him. It was his darkest hour.

Then he knew that he was about to die, and he cried out, "It is finished! Father, into your hands I entrust my spirit!"

Jesus of Nazareth was dead.

# Chapter 28

*Jesus Rises Again*

There came a man called Joseph of Arimathaea. He was a friend of Jesus, and he wanted to take him down from the cruel cross, and put him in a tomb in a beautiful garden.

Pilate said he might take Jesus, and Joseph wrapped the poor, ill-used body in sweet-smelling linen into which fragrant spices had been put. Then he took Jesus to the cool cave in the garden where no one had ever been buried before. He laid Jesus there, and then left the tomb sadly, rolling a heavy stone across the entrance to seal up the doorway.

Some women who loved Jesus saw where Joseph had put him. "Let us come here again as soon as we can," they said to one another. "We can do so little for Jesus now – but we can bring sweet spices to the cave and anoint him, remembering him with love and grief."

So, early in the morning of the third day, these women set out for the garden where the tomb of Jesus was.

"I know where the cave is," said one woman. "There is a big stone outside to seal up the doorway."

"Shall we be able to move the stone?" said the other

women, in dismay. They entered the garden and went to
the tomb.

There was no stone in front of the cave! Someone had
moved it. The women were full of astonishment, and
they went fearfully inside the cave.

The body of Jesus was gone – but there, sitting in the
tomb, was what they thought was a young man, dressed
in a long and dazzling white robe.

All the women looked at him in fear and wonder. Who
was this beautiful young man? Where was the body of
Jesus?

The young man saw their fear. "Do not be afraid!" he said. "Are you looking for Jesus of Nazareth, he who was crucified? He is risen. He is no longer here. See, here is the place where his body lay."

The women trembled, thinking this young man, so strange and dazzling, was surely an angel. He spoke again.

"Go on your way," he said. "Go to the disciples of Jesus, and tell them that Jesus will go before them into Galilee, and that they will see him there."

The women could not say a word. They fled away from the cool dark cave, which was so strangely lit by the angel, and hurried out of the garden.

"Jesus has arisen from the dead! Can it be true?" they said. "Was that an angel? He looked like one. What strange words he spoke! Jesus is gone from there, that is plain. Where is he? Has he come to life again?"

They went to the disciples, who had all hidden themselves away in Jerusalem, afraid that they might be caught and punished too. They were frightened, puzzled and unhappy. How could their beloved master have died such a terrible death? Was he not the son of God?

The women came to them, panting out what they had seen and heard. "Jesus has risen again!"

The disciples were full of the utmost amazement and gladness. Could this really be true? Peter and John could not wait for a moment. They ran off to the tomb in the garden as swiftly as they could.

John got there first. He stooped down and looked into the tomb. The angel was no longer there. The body of Jesus was not to be seen. Only the grave-clothes were there, the garments in which Joseph of Arimathaea had so lovingly wrapped the dead Jesus. They were neatly folded in a pile.

"See, Peter," said John. "The women spoke the truth. Jesus has gone. He has risen again! This is glorious news."

They both went into the tomb, marveling. "We must go back and tell the others," said Peter. "Did not our master say that he would rise again in three days' time? This is the third day – and he has in truth arisen!"

"If only we could see Jesus!" said John, longingly. "I would so much like to see our dear Lord again."

# Chapter 29

## *What Happened to Mary Magdalene*

One of the women who had fetched the disciples to the tomb was Mary Magdalene. She had loved Jesus very much, and when the disciples had gone, she stood weeping by the tomb. As she wept, she bent down and looked again into the cave. She now saw two angels there, one sitting where the head of Jesus had lain and the other were his feet had been. They spoke to her gently. "Why do you weep?" they said.

"I weep because they have taken away the body of my Lord, and I do not know where they have laid him," said Mary sorrowfully.

She suddenly felt that someone else was nearby and she turned to find out who it was, blinded by her tears. It must be the gardener. He would know where the body of Jesus was.

"Why do you weep?" said a tender voice. "Whom are you looking for?"

"Oh, sir!" cried Mary, weeping still more bitterly, "sir, if you have taken my lord somewhere, tell me where you have laid him, and I will take him away."

And then the man who Mary thought was the gardener said one word to her in such a familiar, loving
voice that she knew who he was at once.

"Mary!" he said.

Mary looked up at him, crying out joyfully, her eyes
suddenly full of happiness.

"My master!"

She knew that it was Jesus who had come to her, and
she fell on her knees to worship him, a great gladness in
her heart.

# Chapter 30

*The End of the Story*

For forty days Jesus stayed on our earth. He went to his friends and to his disciples, making them happy, and telling them what they must do.

They must spread his kingdom of love, they must tell everyone the good news, they must teach, they must help the weak and the poor – they must carry on the work he had begun.

"You are the beginnings of my Church," he said.

They were the first Christians, the first of the many many millions who were to come.

And then, after forty days, Jesus came to the disciples no more. "He has ascended to heaven in a cloud of glory," they said. "But yet he is here with us still, in our hearts and minds, helping us just as he did when he was alive."

He is here with us too, always ready to help and to comfort. He came down to this world to be one of us and to show us how to be good and loving, the most wonderful man the world has ever seen.

Echoing down the centuries that have passed since Jesus was born, nearly two thousand years ago, still comes his greatest commandment to us and to all men:

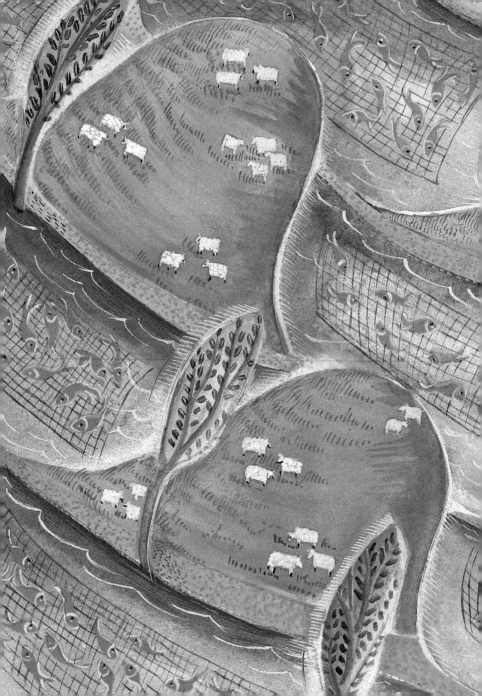